I0833139

Beautifully Transformed

DISCOVERING BEAUTY IN THE BEAST

TACONDRA L. BROWN

Copyright

Beautifully Transformed: Discovering Beauty in The Beast.

Printed in the United States of America.

All scripture quotations are taken from the Holy Bible, New Living Translation, New King James Version, Amplified Bible.

All definitions obtained from Merriam-Webster.com

For information on bulk purchases, please contact us at: info@tacondralbrown.com

Book Cover design by LaQuaila Davis of Vanity Graphics

ISBN: 978-0-9997802-5-1

For You formed my innermost parts; You knit me [together] in my mother's womb. I will give thanks and praise to You, for I am fearfully and wonderfully made; Wonderful are your works, and my soul knows it very well.

Psalms 139:13-14

TABLE OF CONTENTS

Introduction

December 31, 2015

Lord, I'm tired. I'm tired of losing these fights against myself, my husband, my fears, but even more so, against you. Why am I so strong? Why can't I just... surrender? I realize that I am indeed my own worst enemy. As time quickly approaches for the year 2016, I reflect on years passed. All the struggles I've encountered, the tests I've passed and the ones I've failed. The trials I've endured, and the ones I still face. I've come a long way, but I still have struggles, like my inability to be happy with what I see on the outside. This issue has spilled over into my marriage and, although, I know my husband loves me the way I am, I long to experience lasting contentment with myself.

My eyes have been opened to harsh truths about my self-image and the way I love myself. I refuse to live another day or year thinking the same, doing the same things, and living the same way. My mind is made up. I will not be the same in 2016. As I prepare for this weight loss procedure, I pray that this journey will transform my life and enhance my marriage for the better. Father, I pray that you'll use this experience to mature and develop me more; spiritually, mentally, emotionally and physically.

I know it won't be easy and to be honest, I'm scared. But this is a life-changing opportunity I'm not going to talk myself out of. I'm doing it afraid and facing my fear of embracing the unknown. I don't know if I'll suffer or how much, but one thing I do know is that I won't be the same because of this. And guess what Tacondra? That's okay! You don't want to be the same, so use this opportunity to start over.

I'm viewing this surgery as a second chance at life because somewhere along the line 12 years ago I stopped living and started existing. I allowed the pain of my loss and the trauma to leave a scar beyond skin deep. I've let the fear that overtook me years ago hold me back for too long, and I've used the pain as an excuse not to care about myself as I should. Stress has consumed my mind, and my body has suffered. No more! The devil has played with my mind and body long enough! I have decided to trust God even through this process! I believe 2016 and beyond will be the years that God shows himself strong in my life if I am willing to surrender my all to Him.

I know I've said it time and time again, but Father, I surrender all! My heart, my mind, my body, my soul, my marriage, finances, my child, my loss, the hurt and the pain…I surrender my life to you! Have your way in me. Satan you no longer have power over me; therefore, you must flee! It's been a long time coming, but I know in my heart that a change is on the horizon. I will prosper and be in good health, even as my soul prospers (John 3:2). Father, in 2016 and beyond help my soul to prosper. For then and only then will everything else flow and be prosperous in my life.

INTRODUCTION

I'll never forget the years of being a "chubby" caterpillar and the struggle of relinquishing one form for the other while transforming into a beautiful butterfly. In my first book "Transformed from Pain to Purpose" I shared my story about giving birth to my daughter at the age of 18, bleeding profusely while delivering her, and as a result losing my womb in the same day. For years the fainted scar that stretches from one side of my lower abdomen to the other reminded me of my barrenness and how people could only see my youthfulness, but they couldn't see the pain of my loss. The shock that left me paralyzed with fear, shame, and an unhealthy state of mind. Not only was my mental and emotional condition poor, but my body became my worst enemy, and food became one of my best friends.

Living with menopause as a young woman was a nightmare; hot flushes, sweats, irritability, mood swings, hormonal acne, and unexplainable weight gain merely topped off a load of depression I was fighting. Pounds of guilt, shame, pain, low self-esteem and self-worth parked themselves around my waistline, and everywhere else it was non-existent before. The weight seemed to never go away regardless of how much I exercised or ate healthily. Plateaus and weight regain trailed my successes, and even then, I wasted thousands trying to maintain what little weight I could keep off. Discouragement and disappointment got the best of me until I'd just give up.

I'd eat anything that satisfied my imaginary appetite, helped suppress the memory of my loss, and kept me from dealing with the negative emotions I dared not to confront. As years passed and rapid changes in my body occurred, I developed a love-hate relationship with food and myself. I resorted to emotional eating at best just for relief from hopelessness. Being content with who I was as a person and my appearance seemed impossible.

One day I'd look in the mirror, and like what I see then the next I couldn't stand the sight of walking past my own reflection. My soul was broken on the inside, but I wore a mask on the outside to conceal my misery. I was a walking dead person, portraying happiness, confidence, and the appearance of wholeness on the outside without even fully understanding what being *whole* meant, and I was screaming for help on the inside. These masks offended the truth about who I was but fulfilled the appearance of who I imagined people thought I should be. Disguising pain becomes easy when you've mastered looking strong for so long.

I wouldn't dare talk to a therapist about my misery because "*no one would understand or connect with my loss,*" unless they'd experienced a loss like it themselves. So, I named stinking thinking my therapist and prescribed isolation as the treatment for my pain. The woman behind the mask became a BEAST. She was **B**roken, **E**mbarrassed, **A**bandoned, **S**ad, and **T**imid, though no one could really see it.

Then there was the woman inside of the beast. A woman bound by chains of fear and held captive against her own will. She yearned for freedom and for the radiance of God's light to shine upon her face, but her true identity was buried beneath the dark soil of a hardened heart, sadness, pounds of pain, unforgiveness, anger, bitterness, and resentment.

In secret, this woman envisioned herself as an unstoppable bold warrior princess with strength to help others more than herself. She thrived in every endeavor and wasn't afraid to be her true self; She appreciates peaceful environments, enjoys listening to all kinds of beautiful music, the sound of birds chirping, the wind blowing, ocean waves crashing and waterfalls flowing puts a smile on her face and calms her soul. She delights in experiencing new things in life and explores parts of the world she's never been to through foods.

Occasionally, she adventures off to places unheard of in her mind for an exotic getaway. Giving, encouraging, uplifting, comforting, and speaking life into others and dead things fulfill her. Utilizing her voice for the homeless, abused and disadvantaged gives her voice meaning.

This woman's name is Beauty, and often, she'd surface from the bottomless pit of despair to display the splendor of God's glory resting dormant in her. Others gaze in awe of this bright light projecting from her that she is oblivious to. Fear of the light often thrusts her back into a hole of darkness where lies shout that she is a *nobody*, *inadequate*, *unqualified*, and that there isn't a place for her in this world. All the while, her faith whispers, "BELIEVE! You are more than enough, qualified, loved, wanted, needed, and God has a place and a purpose just for you!" Fear was the comfort zone she fought to escape until a beautiful transformation took place. Over time, her identity was restored, and it forced her into another realm of faith she never knew existed.

You are Beauty. I am Beauty. The Beauty I'm referring to is more than skin deep. Beauty is evolving, embracing, and becoming the woman God created you to be, regardless of what life has done to you and what society says you should do, be, and look like. Beauty matters inside and out; however, it's unfortunate that we live in a culture that worships physical beauty and pressures women and men to look and be a certain way. Many of us measure our worth by how we look and have this "standard" of beauty in our minds. As a Believer in Christ, I often wonder where this standard of beauty came from and what I was supposed to make of it? Is being beautiful or desiring to look good a sin?

Is having Botox injections to get rid of wrinkles or cosmetic surgery of removing unwanted fat an insult to our Creator? Should we feel guilty or condemned for altering things about our bodies to enhance our appearance and the way we think of ourselves? These are examples of the concerns and questions I uttered when praying to God about my decision to have weight loss surgery after struggling for years. The subject of being beautiful and saved wasn't discussed often when I was growing up. Especially not in church. Many of us heard what *not* to wear or how *not* to look in church, others have even been led to believe that beauty leads to sin or causes others to sin and that it can only be vain or self-centered to talk about.

Why do we struggle with the idea of physical beauty? And how do we get a balanced perspective of it so that God's beauty can shine through us? Beauty isn't just a "look", it's a state of mind.

I don't claim to have all the answers, but I hope to provide insight and a new perspective about beauty, both physically and spiritually. I shared my story from pain to purpose and how God healed and transformed my heart and mind spiritually, but this is another layer of my journey from the inside out. You see, my spiritual transformation began on the inside but was refined and perfected as my outside appearance changed. In fact, what was happening inside of me had to catch up with what I was becoming on the outside. Transforming requires you to un-become what you were in order to become who you are meant to be! It's not an easy or comfortable process, but it is a beautiful journey. Honestly, it's still a complicated process for me; however, it's not impossible to go or grow through.

As you traverse your beautiful journey of transformation, understand that your process may not look like mine or anyone else's, and that is very much okay! Just like a caterpillar changes into a butterfly, you too must transform into the person God formed you to be long before He ever placed you in your mother's womb. Abba Father already sees you in that state and determined what your destiny would be from the beginning. Life experiences, good and bad, have the power to shape or alter your beliefs and the truth of God's Word if you aren't secure in your faith and in His promises.

The words penned in this book are to remind you of the beauty living inside of you regardless of the circumstances you've endured or may encounter in life that make a beast out of you. No matter how ugly life gets on the outside the beauty inside never fades, you must dig to rediscover it. I can only share my point of view with you. This is my testimony, and I hope my truth and transparency inspires and encourages you. As always, it is my prayer that this book will add value to your life and help frame your focus of God's vision of you. I hope you're prepared to laugh, smile, and cry on this small journey with me, again! Are you ready? I am, let's go!

My Journey

MY JOURNEY

I know firsthand the dangers of unresolved pain. Internalizing pain can result in your body expressing grief in other forms such as stress, headaches, extreme weight gain or weight loss and a variety of other symptoms. What you refuse to express taking place internally, will eventually manifest itself externally. My body became my worst enemy after having the hysterectomy, suppressing my pain, and not properly taking care of myself. I didn't know what kind of changes to expect in my body nor was I educated on how to live with menopause at such a young age.

I was merely told I no longer had a womb to carry a baby physically and would need a surrogate if I ever wanted more children. I wasn't advised to seek counseling or therapy to process the trauma of nearly losing my life after birthing my daughter. No one talked to me about it or even asked how I felt about losing my womb. What happened, happened and what was done was done. Honestly, at that time, worrying about those things was the least of my concerns. Being a mom to my daughter, a wife and military spouse to my husband was my priority.

As time went on, the shape of my body began changing into a round apple-like figure. The weight no longer spread evenly across my body like before. Looking at myself in the mirror for longer than five minutes or letting my husband touch me in certain areas became uncomfortable. I even lost the desire to consummate with him because I was embarrassed and ashamed. Every doctor I consulted about my weight simply glossed over the fact that I was menopausal in my 20's because all they could see was my youthful appearance. "Eat right and exercise" became the solution for every issue with my body, a body that was altered from its original state years prior.

They never discussed hormonal treatment or therapy options, never ran any tests or even verified if I had a womb and ovaries or not, for that matter. I felt as though the doctors didn't want to help me, so I stopped going to them, and I started visiting weight loss clinics.

Diet prescription pills, B-12 injections, and whatever appetite suppressants I could use in conjunction with exercise to lose the weight are what I flocked to. I'd lose 20 pounds and gain 30 pounds back as soon as I got off the pills. I found myself in this cycle of losing and gaining weight using diet pills, and although the process was frustrating, it didn't stop me from going back to buy more though. I later developed heart palpitations accompanied by chest pains as a result of taking the prescriptions. My optimal weight before giving birth to my daughter and having a hysterectomy was around 170lbs. I was an active softball player for most of my youth so, I'd like to imagine that I was somewhat in shape. Yet, there I was weighing at around 245lbs looking in the mirror asking myself, "*How did I get here*?" Of course, other factors led to me gaining weight besides hormonal and metabolic disorders.

Apart from emotional eating, I was diagnosed with Polycystic Ovarian Syndrome (PCOS) which leads to body hair growth, acne, and—you named it—weight gain. I was also a borderline diabetic, suffered from hypoglycemia, low iron and calcium, and had a few scary episodes that landed me in the emergency room a few times. You're probably thinking, "I thought you had a total hysterectomy?" I did. A total hysterectomy involves removing the uterus (womb) and the cervix, not the ovaries. That is called a "complete hysterectomy." One of my ovaries was removed according to my medical records, and a small piece of my cervix was left inside when they performed the hysterectomy.

Let's just say, I didn't know what was left inside of my body back then and I started not to care about everything else. PCOS affects many women and makes it difficult for the body to use the hormone insulin, which helps convert sugars and starches from foods into energy. [2] Can you guess what my diet consisted of a lot during this time? Yes, sugars and starches. Chocolate, bread, pasta, rice, potatoes, and oh, did I mention bread? I'm a country girl, and I love eating yeast rolls!! You can have the mashed potatoes, just don't take my bread away from me! If you're laughing, that means you can relate.

On a more serious note, if you have problems experiencing any of the following symptoms and haven't been diagnosed with **PCOS**, then you may want to consider doing some research and visiting with your primary care physician for more information:

1. **Constant weight loss struggles**
2. **Fertility issues**
3. **Lower abdominal pains on the sides**
4. **Irregular periods (or no periods)**
5. **Problems sleeping or feeling tired often**
6. **Headaches**
7. **Acne or oily skin**
8. **Unwanted hair growth in certain areas or Hair loss.**

There is no cure for PCOS; however, it can be treated. In my case, I ended up having the one ovary I had left removed due to a cyst the size of a golf ball being attached to it. Going back under the knife was the last thing I wanted to do, but the pain was excruciating so, the doctor recommended it in my case. After having that procedure, I gave up the weight loss pills and committed to working out and eating better.

LIFESTYLE CHANGES

Abba surely has a sense of humor! I met a young lady my age while interning at a homeless shelter that I was serving at in order to complete my college degree. She was also finishing her college internship. Her name is Dominque. Turns out, neither one of us were fond of each other at first. She was not the type of person I'd hang out with, and I could tell I wasn't the type she was used to. But we got along well enough to get the work done and service our clients.

This cumbersome "association" eventually led to us learning more about each other and discovering that we shared the same marriage anniversary date and we both had a daughter named Amiyah. A relationship that was once deemed hopeless, in our minds, turned out to be a weight loss accountability partner, my gym and workout buddy, and eventually a friendship. Dominique was traversing her own weight loss journey during the time and was helping others along their way as a Weight Watchers leader. She coached me, pushed me, and insisted on aggravating me daily at 8am by coming over and making me do insane Beachbody workouts. I thank God for her persistence though, and Turbo Fire! It literally changed my life. I lost about 30lbs by eating healthy, cutting out sugars and starches, drinking protein shakes to replace meals, and by working out consistently. The weight loss wasn't the advantage this time though, it was the lifestyle changes I learned to make. Later, I hired a personal trainer. He tried to kill me, but I learned a lot!

Despite efforts to maintain my new lifestyle changes, I still couldn't break 225lbs. The moment I stop working out four days per week the pounds slowly crept back around my waist, again. That's when I became "over it." I decided I was going to get a tummy tuck and be done with it! Yep, I was going to chop off the problem that wouldn't go away! The day I went for a consultation with a plastic surgeon the doctor asked if I was content with my weight. I told him I wasn't, of course. He then shared that getting a tummy tuck wasn't the best decision for me at that time if I wanted to lose weight.

I told him about my weight loss struggles, and he recommended I go see a bariatric doctor. He also stated the best bariatric surgery to have, in his opinion, was the gastric bypass due to long-term success rates. Truthfully, I wasn't trying to hear what he had to say. I just wanted to get rid of the enormous belly resting on my thighs that was causing a dent in my self-esteem. Again, another quick fix was all I wanted. At the same time, I was afraid to get a whole portion of my body chopped off. For some reason, images of the stitched up female character from the animated movie *The Nightmare Before Christmas* kept coming to mind, and all I could see was one scene in the film where her arm or something was ripped apart and sewn back together. *Awkward, right?* You're probably going to google the movie if you don't know what I'm talking about so, go ahead, look! You'll laugh or have second thoughts about getting a tummy tuck when you see what I'm talking about.

Anyway, after leaving the surgeon, I began praying about weight loss surgery. I got back to my routine of eating healthy and working out, although, I didn't work out as much as I did before. It was months before I even scheduled a consultation at the bariatric clinic. The day I went for the consult I almost walked out, immediately. Men and women were sitting there who were much larger than I was and I'm sure they were questioning why I was even taking up space. This 250lb, 5'7-inch-girl didn't LOOK like her knees, joints and back suffered from the weight she was carrying, but they didn't know my story or my struggle!

I was hurting just as much as they were; physically, mentally, emotionally, and spiritually. I scheduled follow up visits, went and took a sleep apnea test in addition to a few others that determined my condition before meeting with the doctors.

In fact, I skipped out on some appointments for a few months because I still didn't feel like the right fit for the surgery. I was embarrassed and unsettled. I earnestly sought God for direction and His will during this time of waiting, while maintaining the changes I'd made in my life.

Ultimately, I continued with the process months later. I sat in the room with the doctor one day and told her all the reasons why I shouldn't have the surgery, including that I was too small compared to others. She stopped me and said that I was in fact the perfect candidate for the surgery because of my age, metabolic disorder, and the lifestyle changes I'd made. She stated the surgery was ideal for candidates like me, and that the risks for complications was less. It helped ease my mind and I was later referred to a psychologist for an evaluation.

The reason for the assessment is to identify your strengths, to make sure you have a complete understanding of the effects of surgery, and to see if you have a healthy support system in place. It can also identify areas you may need additional support, such as identifying triggers for emotional eating, depression, or a lack of family support. The evaluation is not meant to determine whether you are insane or not. Trust me if you are mad before the surgery, you'll still be crazy afterward.

APPROVED

After the psych evaluation, my file was submitted for approval to my insurance company. My husband was serving in the military during this time, but he was not active duty. Even if you don't understand how military insurance works knowing what I'm about to share is critical to my story. Active duty service members and their family are eligible for what's called Tricare Prime insurance. There are no enrollment fees, copays, or deductibles and the members mostly receive treatment from physicians at military treatment facilities. Referrals are usually required for most specialty care, including weight loss procedures.

Tricare Prime members are also not responsible for filing paperwork or claims.[1] We have Tricare Standard insurance, which is the opposite of everything Tricare Prime consists of.

So, we pay enrollment fees, and monthly insurance premiums like regular people do; although, at a more affordable price. We have copays, deductibles, and don't require referrals for specialty care, and sometimes we file our own claims.

The chances of having a balance after using Tricare Prime insurance was less, whereas, having a bill using Tricare standard was higher. I share this information to lay the foundation for my journey that you will see later confirms, for me at least, that God answered MY PRAYER. Fortunately, I didn't need my primary care physician's referral for weight loss surgery. I was able to go on my own without her approval. I loved my doctor, but she probably wouldn't have given me the referral anyway.

The one company I did need approval from for the surgery was the insurance company! They wouldn't approve me for the Gastric-Sleeve surgery because it wasn't a covered service, but it ended up working out for my good because Rou-N-Y Gastric-Bypass surgery cures acid reflux, which

I had badly. The wait was nerve-racking! You know the feeling you get when applying for a car loan knowing you have subpar credit, and you're hoping someone will take a chance on you and say "yes," and they do? That's the exact feeling I got when the insurance company approved my surgery!

They could have quickly turned me down based on my condition compared to others, but GOD! After the approval, I made my final appointments with the nutritionist while waiting for my surgery date! January 13, 2016 was the big day I was scheduled to have surgery in San, Antonio Texas. I was still nervous, but excited. One thing that lingered was whether I'd have to pay out-of-pocket expenses for the surgery and the hospital stay.

January 5, 2016

It's my 3rd day of dieting before my life changes for the better, prayerfully. January 13 is the "big day." I am excited, nervous, and afraid all at the same time about having weight loss surgery.

I don't know what to expect, and that is the scariest part. But I made a vow that this will be the year I start doing things differently. No more fear.

No more holding back or talking myself out of things that could be for my good. I choose to believe in myself and trust God through this process. I hope I'll learn contentment and experience breakthrough spiritually, emotionally, and physically. Everyone won't understand my struggle or agree with my decision, but that's okay. It's mine. God, please deliver me from people! Teach me through this process how to live a disciplined lifestyle. I believe in my heart that I will be better, stronger, wiser and more beautiful on the outside as I am on the inside. I pray that my marriage and relationships are enhanced. I look forward to becoming the person I've always been inside my heart. Father help me keep a humble spirit and a reverential fear of you.

January 10, 2016

Three more days before I have surgery...I am nervous, excited, and not to forget, afraid! Over the past few days, I've done some soul searching as to why I'm having this procedure done. Honestly, part of me is comfortable being the way I am. I love food and dealing with the thought of not having food, even for just a while, is hard for me to wrap my mind around.

It feels like breaking up with a boyfriend you don't want to let go of. At the same time, I realize just how much food has been a downfall in my life. Food hasn't always been my best friend, although, I've made it my master over the years. I've allowed food to take control over my life and It took having this surgery for me to acknowledge that.

I didn't realize how much of an emotional attachment I had to food. For years, I have masked my pain by resorting to emotional eating. I've run from problems and opportunities that I should have faced and taken advantage of, but instead, I found comfort in eating my way out of problems and into a false idea of happiness.

I'm tired of this love-hate relationship I have with food and feeling sorry for myself. This cycle is coming to an end. I'm ready to take back control of my life. More importantly, I'm willing to love myself MORE. Not to the point of conceit but loving myself the way God loves me; the way my Husband loves me. There's room for one master in my life, and His name is Jesus Christ. I desire to be healthy for years so that I'm better able to serve the Lord, my family, and others. These issues I've been carrying for years in the form of pounds have got to go! I can see it and hear God telling me as the weight falls off, "Let go of every dead weight." Every hurt, pain, and lie the enemy has deceived me into believing ends now! This is my do-over! Father may it be for your glory! I know it won't be easy, but it will be worth it! I'm doing it afraid...

January 16, 2016

Well, I did it! I made it through the Gastric-Bypass Surgery successfully on the 13th. THANK GOD! I slept and walked a lot, for the most part during recovery. Having gas was the most painful, but I have a high tolerance for pain, unlike most people. The scary part was the first nights stay after having surgery my blood sugar levels and my blood pressure spiked sky high. I was given two insulin shots and some other shot for my blood pressure. I thought I was going to die, honestly. I just knew the devil was trying to take me out, again.

Thankfully, they were able to stabilize everything by the end of the following day. I remember feeling regret almost instantly after coming to. I was thinking, "why in the hell did I do this to myself?" I believe I was more upset that I couldn't eat! Although, I didn't even want to eat. The mind games are real! Today, I'm six days post-op, and my energy and strength are much better. I'm still struggling with getting my water intake, but at least I'm holding down fluids well. It's just a matter of drinking them that's the problem! This past Sunday, 1/17/16 I wanted to chew on a piece of meat so badly.

Eric made a dirty rice mix for dinner, and it had hamburger meat in it. I asked Miyah to give me a juicy piece of the scrambled hamburger so I could rub it on my mouth like Chapstick! LOL. I chewed it up enough to get the flavor out of it, then I spat it out. It was like having a piece of heaven! Sad, I know, but the struggle is very real. This journey is going to be a battle psychologically more than anything. It's all in the mind. My mind wants and craves things, but physically I'm not even hungry. It's tempting to try different things I know my body isn't ready for. Talk about will power!

If I didn't have any before, then I'm certainly gaining more each day! I'm currently at 237lbs. According to my records, I've lost a total of 17lbs. Down from 254lbs pre-op, I lost 14lbs on the pre-op diet, and the doctor's records reflect 261 as my highest weight. All in all, I'm grateful for this surgery. Even though it's frustrating and I want to eat! I look forward to what's ahead, and I'm not going to stress myself out about the weight. It will fall off as it needs to!

WEIGHING LESS

Hours turned into days, days turned into weeks, and weeks turned into months. The weight started falling off, and I was enjoying every minute of it. Yes, I had some tough mental days, and there were days when I wanted to eat everything in sight, but I learned to master control of my mind by listening to my body. I followed most of the directions given by the doctors, but I found what worked best for me. I ate the recommended foods from the meal plans provided, took my vitamins and drank my protein shakes daily. If my body rejected something, I went back to what worked until my body was ready to try something new.

There were days I experienced what's called "dumping syndrome," which occurs when you eat foods that aren't easily digested, like sugar for example, and they get dumped from the stomach pouch directly into the intestines too fast. It's the worst feeling in the world, and the symptoms are different for everyone. I get nauseated, my heart starts beating fast, sometimes I break out in sweats, or I get lightheaded, it's just an overall nasty feeling. A feeling that teaches a lesson and benefits the individual in the long run when not ignored. I literally learned how to eat all over again.

After about eight weeks I really started noticing the differences in my body and self-esteem. My energy was better, acne started to disappear, my skin was glowing, and even the color on my elbows started changing (inside joke my husband knows about). I'll never forget the first time I was able to cross my legs without leaning to the side! It was the small victories that made me appreciate this life-changing tool. Especially the things about my marriage that were enhanced! I'll never forget the first time my husband was able to pick me up and carry me to the bedroom! I'd always been substantially heavier than my husband, and it often made me feel more masculine than him. My shoulders were broad like his, my thighs were thick, and I just didn't feel as feminine as I'd wished. All of that changed after the surgery and to this day I enjoy being the smaller and "weaker" vessel.

The surgery did come with its disadvantages though, and I was very aware of them before I made the decision. My hair began shedding around the 5th or 6th month, and it fell out quite often. I wore wigs during this time and made sure to take my vitamins. I started taking Biotin and other vitamins months before I had the surgery to offset hair loss as much as I could, and I believe it helped tremendously.

While the pounds were melting away, there were still moments where I found myself feeling insecure. At times, I'd look at my face and think it was too small or that I looked sickly, I was worried that my husband didn't like my body, and

I even wondered if he felt insecure or threatened by the new stares I was attracting. I also questioned if my daughter would feel insecure about her body as she watched me shrink into her size clothing. All these thoughts stayed in the back of my mind as time went by. Surprisingly, their life also changed for the better as a result. My husband was incredibly supportive and shared plates of food with me whenever we'd go out on dates. He'd order healthy meals just so I could eat without getting sick and he loved that I was a cheap date too! Amiyah and I enjoyed sharing clothes until she had a growth spurt! They both embraced our "newer" lifestyle of eating and we still enjoyed some of our old favorites in moderation. They even lost a few pounds themselves! Talk about a win-win situation!

I remember joining a few bariatric weight loss support groups on social media and after a few months I disconnected from most of them. Some of the groups made me appreciative of my journey, compared to others. Often, I'd scroll down the pages and find people talking about their struggles with complications, slow, little or no weight loss, and even weight gain after having the surgery! Plenty talked about their marriages and relationships falling apart too. Their journeys were not encouraging to me and revealed who was supportive of them and who wasn't. In my own journey, I realized that not everyone will understand, agree with, or even applaud your transformation. Some are inspired, others are intimidated, and many will reveal that they've been who you hoped they weren't all along. The ones who are fine with you when you are in bondage, but the moment you are free and start changing YOU become the problem. Yeah, those type of "*friends.*" It's important to surround yourself with people who will affirm and not afflict you during your transformation process, both spiritually and physically.

It's also essential to maintain or acquire a level of humility as your body and image transform because there is a visible difference between confidence and arrogance. While looking at individual's photos in the groups, I could discern the conceit and vanity. I saw it in the way they dressed and composed themselves in pictures and videos they'd post. It was evident that some weren't used to the new attention and there was a difference between those who were loved and affirmed by their spouses and family members prior versus those who were not. The screams for love, likes, validation, and approval was extremely audible.

Then there were those who displayed their beauty in a way that breathed confidence. You could see that they were entirely convinced of what they and others were already suggesting. They just couldn't see the beauty about themselves in totality. I like to think of myself as one that fell into this category. I still had flaws but held a measure of balance about myself. Finding a healthy balance of too much or too little confidence was the key. From my point of view, weight loss transformation will more than likely magnify what's already inside of you, good or bad. For example, if you were a humble heavy person before losing weight, then the chances are you'll be that ordinary, confident person after losing weight.

The more you love and embrace who you were during your journey, who you are, and who you're becoming you'll gain more confidence in yourself and your ability to flourish. Not much changes about your individuality or style when you already possess some form of confidence in your identity before transforming. On the other hand, if there are voids in your life and areas in your heart in need of healing, brokenness will still be visible even in some of your best selfies.

I thank God for a husband who always affirmed and introduced me to others as his "beautiful wife" before I ever lost one pound. As a result, there was no need for me to go looking for validation in all the wrong places. And receiving compliments still don't go to my head because that was never a cavity needing to be filled in my life. Truthfully, while I am appreciative, I'm sometimes overwhelmed by the flattering remarks that it pushes me into isolation. Notably, during times when my husband is not present to cover me.

Much like my experience with my inability to have more children, I haven't had to wear my choice to have bariatric surgery around my neck like a dog tag to identify the cause of my physical transformation. Most people look at me and don't know I've lost my womb or had weight loss surgery unless I tell them.

Earlier I mentioned the possibility of me having out-of-pocket expenses for surgery was a concern. The hospital charges primarily. The day of surgery I had a $25 co-pay, surprisingly! But it was the major bill I waited anxiously for in the mail. You've probably heard the saying: "If it's God's will it's God's bill." If you haven't, then you just did. I remember opening the envelope from the insurance company with the claim information. My eyes traveled nervously across the lines as pondered how much the surgery and hospital stay turned out to be, and what I owed. The total was $38,000 combined for the operation and hospital charges. I OWED NOTHING! I even waited a few more months for another bill to come just to be sure, and nothing came.

My total out-of-pocket expenses totaled approximately $500-600, which included my psych eval, copays for visits at the clinic, and the cost of a binder and products they "required" for the surgery. Everyone's insurance company is different just like everyone who has weight loss surgery or are considering it circumstances may be different.

By the grace of God, I haven't had any complications since my surgery, nor have I had any setbacks to land me in a hospital somewhere. In contrast, I met a woman who had the same surgery as me on the same day and her story was the complete opposite. She suffered complications and encountered losses in her life after the surgery, though some were for her good. I share that to show not everyone's journey is the same. So, be careful about comparing yours to someone else's. This book isn't just about weight loss surgery or for the person who's considering it. This book is to help you understand that transformation is an inside out process, and that beauty is also a state of mind. You can lose weight and put on your best outfit, squeeze into your tightest waist trainer, beat your face with the fanciest makeup, glue on the most fabulous eyelashes, and throw on your best wig, but it still won't repair a hardened and broken heart, mind, relationship, marriage, spirit and soul.

Inside Out

INSIDE OUT

We often portray an image of our lives and how we honestly feel about ourselves on the outside that doesn't always match what's on the inside. Growing up, it reminds me of hearing my parents and other adults say, "Do as I say, not as I do!" Curious and confused I'd always ask, "why?" And their quick response would be, "Because I'm grown." It's funny because as a mother I have caught myself saying the same thing to my daughter, and that same look of confusion I once had she also had. If you think about it, what are we really telling our kids (if you have them) or better yet, ourselves?

Is it okay for our outside appearance to be deceiving and misleading when it doesn't match what or who we indeed are on the inside? For years I struggled with this very thing; masquerading completeness, joy, and contentment with myself while hiding stuff on the inside out of fear that someone would find me out. Wanting to change but not knowing where to start or even how to go about it. The world teaches us that change happens on the outside and then the inside. But for those of us who believe in Jesus Christ, we know a change must occur on the inside FIRST! We know this but how many of us apply what we know in our lives? "Knowing" will cause you to think but revelation will bring about change in your heart and life. God desires to transform us from the inside out. This happens by studying His word and what He says about us, being processed by the renewing of our minds, learning God's will for us, and by responding in obedience to His way.

While the sinful world around us wants to stunt our growth and keep us wobbling in patterns of dysfunction, disobedience, immaturity, rebellion, and brokenness, God desires for us to be transformed more and more into the likeness of Jesus Christ, bringing about wholeness and completion in us. We all have been guilty at some point or another of portraying our lives to be something for others to see that is far from the truth. We make judgment calls about people based on what we see on the outside without having a clue as to what they are going through internally or have experienced in life. I'll be the first to admit I'm guilty. And if you haven't found yourself judging others or tempted to be something you're not, well, I think you're just in denial, period. It's not a matter of IF you'll do it but WHEN.

Whether you were the rich kid growing up living the dream life in the suburbs or you were the poor kid growing up surviving in the ghetto wishing you could be the rich kid, one thing I am sure of is that we never know the depth of someone's story. The rich kid may have all the beautiful things in life and are well taken care of but missing the love of one or both parents behind closed doors. The poor kid may not have the luxury of eating out every day or having stylish clothes to wear, but the love and nurturing they receive from both parents at home is rich.

The depiction of the *Iceberg illusion* would have us believe those who are successful and live a "fruitful" life have it all together, or never experienced failure. On the other hand, it can cause us to believe those struggling in life is a result of their laziness, lack of focus, and bad choices they've made. We live in a world where two dichotomies exist, meaning there is always a different side to what we see. It's kind of like the sayings: "Everything that glitters ain't gold" and "One man's trash is another man's treasure." They both are right, and they each have opposite sides! Everything that glitters may not be gold, but that one thing that does glitter just might be!

Let me tie this all together for you, at the end of the day we shouldn't easily judge a book by its cover because what looks to be authentic fruit might just be manufactured; looking the part on the outside but falling apart on the inside. You might see someone's success on the surface and never know their struggle or what they've sacrificed to get there. Oppositely, just because someone looks like a failure doesn't necessarily mean they are.

Society screams we must be a quiet failure to have loud success. But what if we're supposed to be a loud failure with quiet success? Do you believe failure is better when hidden? Are you afraid of being a public failure? Perhaps, you're forcing something in your life to prove to yourself or others that you're not struggling? Stop pretending. Stop lying to yourself and stop trying to manufacture a false version of you. The real version of you is always the best version of you. When beginning your spiritual and physical journey of transformation start with the truth! There is nothing you can hide from God. He sees and knows both the exposed and unexposed parts of who you are. God examines our heart and knows everything about us (***See Psalms 139: 1-13***). So, you might as well be honest with yourself. Address any bad areas in your heart and soul and confront your fears your shortcomings. Write down or express your desires, dreams, and overall goals then determine what's holding you back!

My decision to have weight loss surgery was a result of me being honest with myself about my struggle; not just an excuse to look good. The path I chose may not be the best direction for you because there is no one size fits all solution. The best decision of one person's life may be the worst decision ever for another. Regardless of the path you choose, I hope that your transformation first begins on the inside. This process requires looking at yourself in the mirror and confronting the truth about the woman you see.

The Woman You See

THE WOMAN YOU SEE

Who do you see when you look in the mirror? Do you see the woman God fashioned in His mind before forming and placing you inside your mother's womb? Do you see a fearfully and wonderfully made masterpiece? Or do you only know the woman you're unhappy with being right now? Who is the woman staring back at you in the mirror? Do you know what she likes? What her passions are? What does she want to do for fun and what are her favorite foods? What are her deepest fears and greatest desires? What does she believe strongly in and value the most? Do you know what her purpose in life is? If you find it difficult to answer any of these questions, perhaps it's safe to suggest that you don't know who you are, or you only know a corrupt version of yourself.

I'll go a step further and submit unto you it would be difficult to gaze at your reflection long enough for an answer to even cross your mind. This has certainly been my experience. But why? If you grabbed your cell phone right now to take a selfie, the first thing you'd do is fix what's out of place. If you don't believe me, watch what you do the next time you take one! We are quick to notice our flaws before ever acknowledging our perfections. We tend to view ourselves based on our life experiences, what has happened to us, and the condition we are in as a result. *Motherless. Fatherless. Abused. Abandoned. Lonely. Rejected. Trash. Not good enough. Inadequate. Broken. Unworthy. Useless. Unhappy. Ugly. Too dark-skinned. Too fair-skinned. Fat or too skinny,* ____________________ **(you fill in the blank)**.

The losses we encounter, whether it be the death of a loved one, a physical loss, divorce, rape, molestation, or job loss can cause an identity crisis if you aren't secure in who you are. Even if you thought you knew who you were at one point. An identity crisis is "a period of uncertainty and confusion in which a person's sense of identity becomes insecure, typically due to a change in their expected aims or role in society." I experienced a loss of identity. I felt stripped of my femininity and status as a woman when my womb was removed. I lost a part of me that made me feel complete as a woman, even though I gave birth to a child. You may have been molested, raped, or abused and as a result, your identity was lost or stolen. Life happens to all of us but no matter the circumstances, identity crisis has the power to affirm who you already are or introduce you to who you were created to be.

I remember watching the animated movie titled *Moana* and God begin speaking to me prophetically through the scenes. If you haven't already seen the movie, you just received a new homework assignment! WATCH THE MOVIE! It is about A teenage girl who sails out on a daring mission to save her people and their land. In the movie, there is a mother island called Te Fiti (representative of the woman God sees), and her heart held the most significant power ever known. It could create life itself and she shared it with the world. Te Fiti's heart was stolen from her and lost to the sea. Without it, she crumbled and gave birth to terrible darkness, named Te Ka, that spread and drained the life in the sea and everything it touched.

The ancient legend was that the ocean would choose someone to restore the heart of Te fiti to save the lands and its people. Moana was chosen to sail across the open ocean on an action-packed voyage, encountering enormous monsters and impossible odds. Along the way, Moana discovers the one thing she always sought, her own identity. God gave me a powerful revelation through this film that I'd like to share with you. I believe every woman can relate to the four women I saw in this movie or will find themselves in a phase at some point: (1) The woman who doesn't know who she is (Lost woman). (2) The woman behind the mask. (3) The forsaken woman (in the middle). (4) The woman God sees.

THE LOST WOMAN

The woman who doesn't know who she is represents the lost woman. She doesn't know who she is because she doesn't know WHOSE she is. There's a still small voice that calls her, but she is unable to recognize who is calling, why she's being called, or what she's being called to. All kinds of barriers, distractions, people, and doubts prevent her from trusting and obeying the voice inside; however, the thirst to fill an empty void inside of her won't go away. She has questions and is searching for answers. She's looking for something to give meaning and purpose to her life. When this woman looks in the mirror, she feels lost, nameless, incomplete, purposeless, unvalued, unloved, unrecognized, misunderstood, embarrassed, and she often compares herself to others. I'm reminded of the Samaritan Woman Jesus met at the Well when I think about the characteristics of the lost woman:

1. **She Is "Thirsty" (John 4:7) "she came to draw water").** This woman is searching for something to quench the thirst inside of her, a thirst that Jesus is already aware of.

   Jesus tells the Samaritan woman about this living water He gives that will never cause her to thirst again and she admits she is thirsty in verse 15: "Sir, give me this water! Then I'll never be thirsty again and I won't have to come here to get water".

2. **She Is Misunderstood:** Scholars and most people automatically assume that the Samaritan woman was a prostitute because of the detail in the story where Jesus tells her about the five husbands she's had, and the one she was with was not her husband. A shadow of shame is cast down on her by others. But when researching the 1st-century wives, I found that most women back then were

frequent widows due to the high death rate or they were divorced. God gave me a revelation of a difference about her "thirst". I submit unto you that this woman was not a prostitute looking for a customer, but a religious seeker thirsty for truth and revelation.

3. **She's Curious**: She has questions about her purpose in life and is in the process of discovering who she's meant to become.

Is this woman you? What God wants you to know:

- ♥ You are a child of God (**John 1:12**)
- ♥ You are God's temple and that God's spirit lives in you (**1 Corinthians 6:19**)
- ♥ God loves you and has chosen you (**1 Thessalonians 1:4**)
- ♥ You have been made complete in Christ Jesus (**Colossians 2:10**)

WOMAN BEHIND THE MASK

The Samaritan woman can also relate to the woman behind the mask. This woman wishes to be invisible, so she hides things that she's ashamed of to keep others from knowing who she really is underneath all the debris of her past. The beautiful smile she wears on the outside conceals her pain, fears, and her struggles. She envisions this great woman God is calling her to be, and she often reveals this person for others to see. She dreams of motivating thousands with her life and her words, and she desires to be an example of change others need to see. But behind the mask, a slave to fear, failure, and the unknown rests. She attempts walking on water with Jesus time and time again, but unbelief, the cares of the world, fear of being judged, and the pressure of pleasing others and God is more than she can bear. So, she gives up.

When this woman looks in the mirror, she feels empty, barren, and fruitless. The scars of her past, the feelings of unworthiness, and a history of shortcomings remind her that she's not good enough. She questions God's call and begs Him to choose someone else. She hides from people and from God, but no matter how deep the grave she tries to throw herself in, God is continuously digging her out. Tugging at the mask she wears, compelling her to uncover the treasures within and to display the beautiful work He's created in her that can transform the lives of many. **Is this woman you? God Wants You to Know:**

The mask is only disguising your pain and covering the beauty of what God created. Remove the veil. God wants to restore you, confirm you, and establish you but you must first be transformed (progressively changed) by the renewing of your mind (**Romans 12:2**).

- ♥ The hardening of your mind has been removed in Christ. Open your mind! (**2 Corinthians 3:14**)
- ♥ You are free in Christ Jesus (**John 8:36**)

THE FORSAKEN WOMAN

This woman is not necessarily in search of who she is or hiding from God nor has she fully tapped into being the woman God sees, although she's completely aware of who she is. This woman is at a point in her life I'd like to call "the middle". It is the place where most feel forgotten about. (i.e. middle child). It's the place where life happens; suffering, heartache, pain, doubt, and oftentimes a loss of faith occurs. The middle is defined as "**the point at or around the center of a process**".

When this woman looks in the mirror, she sees all that she has given, and all that life has taken from her. She sometimes questions and doubts her efforts and all that she's done or is doing to become better: A better friend, wife, mother, teacher, a better version of herself. This woman desires to have more, be more, and do more in life, but she feels stuck. Whispers of doubt and the comfort of settling restrain her, the smoke from past disappointments, pain, heartache, guilt, and shame hardens her heart and clouds her ability to see herself giving life to what's slowly dying inside of her.

She may feel useless, resentful, bitter, frustrated like she's at war within herself or with others, she may not have the desire to be productive. She finds herself angry with God as she questions "Why have you forsaken me?" But all she hears is silence. The "middle" is the place where life happens; suffering, heartache, pain, and often a loss of faith occurs. Most felt weak and forgotten about at this point, but it's really where God's power is made perfect and where our faith is made stronger. **Is This Woman You? God Wants you to know:**

In the middle is where preparation takes place. It's where you become refined, purified, and tested before receiving the blessing. Know that God is with you and will never forsake you.

- ♥ I am with you always to the very ends of the age (Matthew 28:20)
- ♥ I Will Never Leave you nor forsake you (Deuteronomy 31:6)

THE WOMAN GOD SEES

I am a visual learner, so I love how Jesus uses parables and analogies in the bible to help us understand. A clear depiction of the Forsaken Woman versus the Woman God see's is shown at the end of *Moana*. Even the lyrics of the songs were fitting! I admonish you to watch the movie or at least YouTube the final scene and allow God to speak to your heart. Watch and listen carefully to the words! I will tell you this though, the woman God sees is a precious gift, created in her mother's womb by God's own hand. She is a daughter of the King. The Royal Heir to His divine throne. She Knows WHO she is and WHOSE she is.

People, problems, circumstances, and her feelings don't define her. Stop relying and depending on your emotions to tell you who you are. Feelings will lie to you most of the time. Stop taking on labels that weren't made to fit you: Worthless, useless, powerless, fruitless, desolate, all these things that make you LESS than who you are! God already Knows what's inside of you, He wants YOU to see what's inside of you.

Most of us are likely on a path of figuring out who we are, suffering from a lost or stolen identity, or finally realizing our identity. The way we view ourselves is sometimes broken and misconstrued because we only see what life circumstances and society have turned us into. The image of a beast is slowly painted in our minds; erasing the portrait of beauty God designed. We adopt a corrupted view of ourselves and take on labels of lies that the enemy tries to permanently mark us with, instead of knowing we've already been marked by God.

The word "Zion" is a Hebrew term which means "Chosen by God, distinguished, or marked for your uniqueness." It is also a name often used for the chosen land of Israel or Jerusalem in the Bible (*reference the book of Isaiah).* The central focus of the book of Isaiah is about the city of Jerusalem. God revealed His love for Israel throughout the old testament and made a covenant with the forefathers, Abraham, Isaac, and Jacob about the land and its people. Throughout the book of Isaiah Jerusalem is referred to as the "City of Righteousness" and the "faithful City" (*Isaiah 1: 26*), the "valley of vision" the "city of the Lord", "Zion of the Holy one of Israel" "my delight is in her" (*Isaiah 62:4*), "daughter Zion" (*62:11*), "Sought out" (*62:12*), and "a city not forsaken" (*62:12*).

Jerusalem is God's City, a place sacredly devoted to Him, the city of Zion. God has passion for this beautiful, righteous, fruitful, and faithful city and the people loved God in return. But Jerusalem became corrupt and the people of Israel started rebelling and turning their backs on God. In Isaiah 1:2-27 we are introduced to the "present" or *corrupt* Jerusalem and the "future" or *new* Jerusalem. This is comparable to the woman you see versus the woman God sees. Corrupt versus beautiful. Te-Fiti versus Te Ka in the film, there is powerful revelation in this! In the final scene I want you to pay close attention to what forms around Te Fiti's head!

Remember, Daughter of Zion, you are marked by God and when something is marked or has a sign on it if it is ever lost or misplaced, the sign enables it to be returned to its owner. There is nowhere you could go that God's spirit won't be with you. Even when you get lost, there is no place he wouldn't go to find you and bring you back to Him. You were marked by God before the enemy ever tried to stain you, and there isn't a mark or blemish about you that the blood of Jesus Christ cannot erase.

The power in HIS blood is way more powerful than any circumstance, situation, condition, loss, or lie the enemy will ever throw at you. God's view of you will never change based on what other's think of you or what happens to you. Why? Because He created you, and no person or life situation can alter who God created you to be. Perhaps, with this revelation, you'll get comfortable starring at your reflection just a few seconds longer each day as you begin to love the woman that God loves unconditionally! If you don't take anything else away from this chapter remember this the next time you look in the mirror: **SEE YOURSELF, THE WAY GOD SEE'S YOU!**

Beautifully
Formed

Loving You

LOVING YOU

Do you love your body? Do you take care of yourself physically, emotionally and spiritually? Do you even like yourself? This is probably one of the hardest questions to answer, and in most cases, unfortunately, the answer is "no." I'll be the first to admit I don't always take care of myself physically, emotionally or spiritually as I should. I fall short frequently, and I'm always "trying to get my life," to be honest. Just to make my point of view clear, simply because we don't exercise daily, practice emotional self-care every day, or we miss a morning (or night) of reading our bible doesn't mean we hate ourselves! I recognize that imperfection is part of our human experience. The real issue here is often we don't love the reflection staring back at us in the mirror because of the imperfections we see. How easy is it to focus on your flaws instead of your incredibleness? The more time we spend doing this our self-love tank will always be half-full or empty.

The amount of love we have for our self is often built upon everything and everyone but the one person it should be, Jesus Christ. The measure by which we love ourselves is often based on the love and support we receive from others and the relationships we've been exposed to from a child throughout adulthood. We sometimes base the way we love ourselves off what we can offer others, or vice versa; whether people receive or reject us, and even how people view us. What this truly reveals is a deficiency in us; something's missing or lacking. Deficiencies create a lack of sufficiency in our self-confidence, self-worth, self-image, and the way we love ourselves.

Depending on whether you answered these questions honestly, you'll recognize if loving yourself is a problem or a priority. We often get in the habit of leaving ourselves out of the equation, thinking that loving our self is only about other people and what we can do to make them happy. Understand, there is entirely nothing wrong with loving and caring for others but when it leads to neglecting yourself and beating yourself up for failing to meet everybody else's expectations, or if you allow people's opinions of you to determine your worth then there is a problem. If your answers to any of the questions above do not align with God's Word, this is where the journey of renewing your mind about yourself begins. I'll be transparent with you, just because I authored this book, I speak, preach, prophesy and look like I have it all together doesn't mean I do, or that I feel good about myself all the time. Every day I conceal the blemishes and scars on my face with makeup, and I throw on stylish garments to disguise the imperfections on my body like everyone else. I feel better about myself too! But the best part about being me is when I'm uncovered entirely; when my face is fresh and free of makeup, my hair is messy, I don't have to be dressed up, and I can breathe from not wearing a girdle to keep my kangaroo pouch from showing.

You're probably laughing at my comment, but it's the truth! The image we present for others to see as an outside expression of who we are doesn't always reflect or come close to who we are, the woman we see, or the woman God sees. It's easy to look the part and not be the part; to look rich and not be rich; to appear happy and not really be *satisfied*, or to look holy and not be living holy! *Ouch!* These examples might not be fitting for you or your story; however, I'm almost sure you can fill the line with cases most appropriate for you. None of us are perfect (I most certainly am not) but we were created in the hands and image of perfection. Here are a few points to ponder as you begin exercising loving yourself more.

Self-love encompasses practicing:

1. **Self-Care:** Mentally, emotionally & physically.
2. **Self-Compassion:** Showing and giving yourself the same amount of care, kindness, concern, and grace that you extend to others.

SELF-CARE

What you love you will or should always take care of, period. For example, it's natural for a mother to care for her children because she loves them. *Not all mothers do, but most of them do anyway.* It ought to be natural for a wife to give attention to her husband by meeting his needs, helping him, and caring for him in ways that show she loves him, right? Well, it's difficult to effectively do for others what you won't even do for yourself. Don't confuse what you do for others out of obligation or responsibility with what you choose to do out of love for them. The more passion you have for someone or something, the more love and care you will put into doing whatever it is you do for it or them.

The same goes for our relationship with Christ and even how we love and care for ourselves. On a scale of 1 to 10 (1 being the lowest) what is your level of passion for Christ? Do you even have a passion for yourself? When traveling on a plane, the first thing the stewardess tells you to do if there's a pressure change in the cabin is to, "Put the face mask on yourself first then assist others!" MAMA's, this even applies to you and your precious babies! If you love you, be intentional about taking care of you first, mentally, emotionally and physically, so that you can efficiently care for others.

Living with a mental condition such as depression can easily cause self-care to fall by the wayside. Depression is so real and is not something anyone should have to fight alone. I've battled depression alone, and by the grace of God he met me where I was and brought me out on many occasions. It's imperative that you get the support you need by opening your mouth and acknowledging your condition. Seek treatment that's best for you, whether it's counseling, therapy, or even medication. Just be intentional about bettering your mental health.

Here are five ways to take care of your overall mental health:

1. Reduce stress in your life.
2. Master the art of saying "No" to added stressors.
3. Keep a mood Diary (***Journaling helps with self-awareness***).
4. Surround yourself with positive influences (**Supportive friends & family, new people, environments etc.**)
5. Engage in healthy therapeutic activities (***Relaxation, exercise, walks on the beach, enjoy nature, etc.***)

Again, surrounding yourself with people who affirm you instead of afflicting you is imperative on both your spiritual and physical journey of transformation. Not only is there is a correlation between how we feel and the foods we eat but there is a link between how and what we eat, and the way think of ourselves and our relationship with God. What I share is not meant to be a stumbling block to you. I'm still a work in progress, just like you, just like most of us are. So, believe me when I tell you I'm not boldly preaching to you about something I'm not actively pursuing in my own life. **KEYWORD: Pursuing**! Even in my pursuit of doing better, I'm still human. I stumble and fall and make all kinds of mistakes, but I do my best to get back up and move forward. I'm sharing the revelation Abba Father gave that convicted and set me free! You may have your own convictions, and the Holy Spirit will lead you into all truth and freedom accordingly, but I have a responsibility to release this revelation. I pray that the Holy Spirit will provide illumination for you that leads to application in your life! Knowing better requires us to do better, be better, and make every effort to live better!

View your body as a beautiful gift from God and remember that it hosts your spirit. Wanting to honor your body, also honors God. 1 Corinthians 3:16 declares, "Don't you know that you yourselves are God's temple and that God's Spirit dwells in your midst?" What you put in your "temple" has full impact on your health, physically, emotionally, mentally, and spiritually. The saying, "You are what you eat" is spot-on. So, what does your appetite reveal about you? When you're feeling moody and miserable or happy and lucky what's the first food you run to or crave? I mean, I get it, we all have our days but for some of us, our "days" seem to never end like run-on sentences in a paragraph. I challenge you to examine your heart, emotions, beliefs, and attitudes as it relates to your body and the foods you eat. Perhaps, you've made food an idol in your life and don't realize it. If food, especially unhealthy food, is your first resort instead of the last option you run to when problems arise in life, then you have made it your God. Overeating won't ease the pain, feelings, or negative emotions you refuse to reveal or confront head on. Unhealthy food certainly can't heal you! Only God can do that. Repent and ask the Holy Spirit to help guide you towards living a healthier lifestyle if you feel led. Revelation should cause a change in our hearts; however, revelation without practical application and discipline changes nothing in our lives.

LOVE

Your Worth

YOUR WORTH

God loved you so much that He gave His only Son as a ransom for your soul. Now, I don't know about you but, I often questioned who in my life would sacrifice their own just for me to live? I believe my husband would, after all, he is a solider and has put his life on the line three times serving on combat tours to protect our freedom. Then and again, I would never know until the opportunity presents itself, w*hich by the way, is totally NOT an opportunity I want or need,* just to be clear! Before and even after I became an author or a rising woman of influence, I didn't know my true worth despite having a husband and others who saw something valuable in me. I allowed my loss, feelings of inadequacy, validation from others, and my condition to determine my worth. I never saw myself as one of importance or worthy of being invested in. Hard to believe, right? I bet you can relate to some of the same feelings or at one point you have, right?

Are you quick to run away or recommend someone more capable than you, in your eyes, when asked to accomplish a task? Is it easier to identify the value in everyone else but yourself? It was for me. When the enemy whispered lies that I was worthless, inadequate, incompetent, and incapable of being used to achieve anything significant on my own, I believed him. These lies became my truths and damaged my self-worth. As a result, I found myself searching for my worth in jobs, opportunities, and sometimes people instead of going directly to my Creator.

Selling Mary Kay products, Avon, Soap bars, jewelry, bags, fancy pots or whatever else I could get my hands on was a go-to for me because all I had to do was test the quality, and if I saw value in using the products it was easy for me to convince others. If not, I didn't bother wasting my time. Half the time I ended up buying the products for myself and not selling them at all. I'll explain why I did this below in more detail. But allow me to walk you through my process of realizing issues with my self-worth. I imagined it would be easier for me to sell a product someone else had already assigned a value to, but I was wrong. What I've discovered is whether one sells a product or a service, consumers are more likely to buy into people of worth. People who know their worth!

For example, I sold cookware for a direct sales company I absolutely loved, and I valued the quality of products they offered. I joined forces with some friends of mine who introduced me to the cookware, and I learned how to do the presentations that sold me into purchasing. Performing was never a problem for me but, selling was.

I'm an introvert by nature, but I know how to be extroverted when necessary, therefore, talking to people was never an issue once I opened my mouth. I've always been able to find common grounds with people, like them, and get them to like me in return. But I struggled with asking people for "the sale" and facing my fear of rejection. I thought if I presented a quality product and convinced them of the value in it, they would either buy it or not. Pressuring or forcing someone to purchase something they probably needed but didn't want, or couldn't afford at the time, was not my thing. Still isn't, even if there is value in the product. In the end, I cut myself short every time because, although, I knew the customers loved the cookware and my presentations, I silently questioned whether I was enough for them to buy into or even to buy from? This resulted in little or no sales at all for me.

You see, my confidence in the quality, value, or worth of the product being sold was never the problem. The problem was that I didn't know how to market or sell myself. Why? Because I didn't know the quality I possessed. In fact, the very reason I purchased most of the products for myself instead of trying to sell them to others was because those "things" gave me a sense of worth. I thought filling my hands and my environment with beautiful, high-quality, expensive things would make me feel more valuable.

I'm not saying you shouldn't seek business opportunities best for you or that you can't have nice things, but don't allow those things and opportunities to become idols or cover-ups for your low self-esteem. Imagine yourself as a product or a service being sold to customers. Think about the gifts, talents, abilities, experiences, expertise, wisdom, knowledge, and every hidden treasure inside of you that is valuable to so many around you and in this world. See yourself as the top-shelf quality you are. Now, answer this: **what price are YOU willing to pay for yourself?**

If you answer this question truthfully, the reality about your self-image and sense of worth is revealed. If you can't answer this question, or struggle with knowing your worth, it's time to confront every lie with the truth of God's word concerning you! Your worth must come from seeing yourself through the eyes of Abba Father, not your own. Your worth isn't determined by what you see in the mirror, the size pants you wear, the expensive brands or luxurious environments you surround yourself with, nor is it limited to what others think you. Only the Creator knows how valuable His creation is. Our Heavenly Father determined our worth long ago before the foundations of this earth were ever formed; before He formed us in our mothers' womb. Let's go to the Word of God and see what He has to say about our image and worth!

A GOD-WORTH & IMAGE

Say This Out Loud: MY WORTH IS INFINITE!

Yes, your worth is infinite! Countless! Immeasurable! And without boundaries! There is no limit to your worth from God's point of view. It's one thing to read about what God's Word says about you, but it's another to apply His truths to your life. Knowing something will cause you to think but, again, revelation and illumination of God's Word brings about change in your heart and life. Many of us have the knowledge about God's Word concerning our worth, but we can't birth or manifest these truths in our lives due to having spiritually dead or perverted wombs. We don't have the capacity to carry! Sometimes, there is no worth in dead things.

In my case, having a spiritually dead womb gave the enemy free range to play with my mind and abort every seed of truth and life planted inside my spirit before it could bear fruit. By the grace of God, my spiritual womb has been replaced, revived, and my mind renewed, transformed and made alive through Christ! Having a healthy self-image is essential to pursuing what God has for you. Allow me to share with you one of the many revelations God revealed to me regarding self-image.

Scripture tells us that God said, "Let us make human beings in our image, to be like us. They will reign over the fish in the sea, the birds in the sky, the livestock all the wild animals on the earth, and the small animals that scurry along the ground." So, God created human beings in His own image, In the image of God he created them; male and female He created them" (Genesis 1:26-27". These two verses of scripture are so powerful and significant. Our triune God (the Father, Son, and Holy Spirit) made you and I according to His likeness. Not in a physical sense, but a spiritual and moral sense. Likeness is defined as: "the fact or quality of being alike; resemblance".[1] God is Spirit, and spiritually we were created in His image and likeness. Hebrews 2:7 tells us we were created a little lower than the angels and crowned with God's glory and honor.

Keep in mind, Angels are celestial; they were created to live and exist in the sky (or Heaven), although they can come to earth. When God formed man from the ground and gave him an earthly body, which is just an outer shell of flesh, man did not become a living being (soul) until God breathed His Spirit (*Pnuema*) into him. Therefore, we are a physical representation of God (The Father). What I need for you to understand and get into your spirit is that God thought so highly of you that He created Heaven on earth. **YOU ARE HEAVEN ON EARTH**!

If you're a mother and can remember what it felt like to behold the beauty of your newborn baby after carrying him or her for nine long months and the hours of exhausting labor; or if you've tasted or experienced something so pleasant that all you can compare it to is "heaven on earth," then hopefully you'll understand my point. Some things on earth are just priceless, and you, my beautiful butterfly, are one of them. When you understand the value in knowing what your loving, caring and sharing Heavenly Father thinks about you, how much He loves you, and the thoughts He thinks towards you, your "state of mind" will change. You will see yourself from God's perspective, you'll appreciate who you are, and the way God made you; not what life has made you.

You won't discount your worth as a person or belittle the value of your voice and the message God has given you to carry throughout this earth. Diminishing the value of the gifts, talents, treasures and the message God has placed inside of you is an insult to God and says that you don't value the Holy Spirit within you, especially if you proclaim to be a Believer. It doesn't matter what you have gone through in life or what the lies the devil wants you to believe, you may have been damaged, but your worth is never diminished! Most importantly, you'll realize how beautiful you are, inside and out! God created you with beauty in mind. So, you see it's true, BEAUTY IS A STATE OF MIND! Not just an outward appearance. Below are more scriptures I want you to study the following scriptures, meditate on them, and journal about your worth and beauty from God's perspective:

- Psalms 139: 13-16 (**Fearfully and wonderfully made**)
- Ephesians 1: 3-4 (**God chose you & made you worthy of all spiritual blessings**),
- Ephesians 1:13-14 (**You are God's possession**)
- John 3:16 (**God Loves you SO MUCH**)

I challenge you to find more scriptures that minister to your heart about God's view of your worth.

Write them here:

Conclusion

CONCLUSION

My outward appearance changed after having weight loss surgery, but it was the transformation that took place internally no one could see that mattered the most. It was the most difficult, uncomfortable, painful, yet, rewarding process. It certainly didn't happen overnight either! I'm still growing and going through renovations in my heart, mind, body, and soul, daily. I'm still a work in progress, we all are. My advice is for you to make the most of your journey, don't skip out on parts of the process, and don't take it for granted because your journey isn't even about you, it's to help someone else! Allow God to transform you beautifully from the inside out, and never forget the struggle you endured to get "there." A butterfly never forgets it was once a caterpillar, but it will never fly high in its glory continuing to think like one. There is no glory in transforming into a butterfly if your mind remains in bondage and you continue living in dysfunction.

I knew that feeling better about myself and looking better was a benefit of the surgery, but I never imagined my transformation, internally and externally, being a gift from God. I don't say that conceitedly because beauty is a gift that comes from the Lord. It flows from Him because He is beautiful (*Psalms27:4*). The Bible references scriptures about beauty and characters who were described as beautiful. Sarah, the wife of Abraham, was so beautiful and desirable even in her old age that he lied about who she was to him and gave her to Pharaoh *(Genesis 12)* and later to a Canaanite king just to keep himself alive *(see Genesis 20)*.

Esther was beautiful and chosen as Queen to replace Vashti. Her beauty was a conduit that led to saving her people! How powerful is that! Rebecca, the wife of Isaac, was also beautiful (*Genesis 24:16)*. These are a few examples of the gift of beauty spoken of in the Bible, but there is also an ugly side to it when misused and separated from the Giver. Lucifer was the seal of perfection (created in the image of God), full of wisdom, and exquisite in beauty (Ezekiel 28:12). The devil is the prime example of how beauty apart from God can turn ugly when it is idolized and used against God. Pride became his downfall because he wanted what didn't belong to him, the glory of God.

One day, I was in the shower, and I distinctly heard God say, "I'm looking for Diadems, not Divas." Perplexed by this statement, I researched the definitions of diva and diadem then it made sense! Society paints the image of a diva as a female performer or talented singer; however, a diva is defined as a "self-important person that is temperamental and difficult to please." On the other hand, a Diadem is a type of crown, symbolic of God's sovereignty, power and glory. What powerful revelation! Women have been taught to use the term "Diva" so loosely and with pride! We label ourselves and our daughters as divas without knowing what it really means! It's important that we do our research and educate ourselves or else we will fall victim to word curses! Remember, lucifer was a self-important angel, and God did away with him! Abba Father wants to display His glory through diadems on this earth, not divas! So, which one are you?

A desire to be beautiful is not wrong or unwomanly, but there is nothing attractive about a vain, exposed, prideful, self-important woman with goods but no glory. Real beauty is more than just a beautiful body or a pretty face, it's of the soul. There is a beauty to be admired and sought after first, which is a quality of the mind and heart and in deed and service. True beauty is a gift from God for God!

In sharing all of this I want to be clear, I'm not encouraging you to go and have weight loss or cosmetic surgery just to feel better about yourself. That is not the point of sharing my journey, but instead, to encourage you on your own transformational journey with Abba. No matter what decision you make, it's going to cost you something. What are you willing to sacrifice? Whether it's late nights and early mornings in the gym or sacrificing eating solid foods for chicken broths and protein shakes only for months, it will cost you. Bariatric surgery is not an easy way out of doing the "hard work" to lose weight, although, this seems to be portrayed that way by most people. And those who choose that route, for the right reasons, are prejudged without knowing their story.

Perhaps, knowing mine has given you new perspective. I've often been asked if I could choose to have the surgery over again would I do things differently?

My answer to that is this: If I could choose to have my womb again, I would gladly accept that gift. In the same light, God gave me a gift by way of bariatric surgery that I never imagined would enhance and transform my life the way it has. He literally gave me the gift of BEAUTY, inside-out. What the devil means for our bad God always turns it around for our good and His glory!

If you are considering weight loss surgery because of a condition you are in, I advise you to seek the Lord in prayer, consult your physician, and check your heart and motives. IT IS NOT EASY! Nor is it meant for everyone! Above all else I want you to remember this: You Are **B**old; you are **E**nough; you are **A**ffirmed by God; you are **U**nstoppable and no matter what, always remain **T**rue to **Y**ou! The **BEAUTY** in you!

I hope you've been inspired to see yourself in a different way, the way God sees you! You are beautiful, precious, a royal diadem in the hand of God, a crown of glory and a display of His sovereignty; You are worthy, loved, chosen, wanted, and a priceless gift in God's sight! Keep digging until you **Discover all the Beauty inside the Beast.**

References

My Journey

1. http://www.militaryspot.com/benefits/tricare-standard-vs-prime

2. https://www.webmd.com/women/polycystic-ovary-syndrome-pcos-and-weight-gain#1

3. What Is Insulin Resistance? | POPSUGAR Fitness. https://www.popsugar.com/fitness/What-Insulin-Resistance-44701766

The Woman You See

1. https://www.imdb.com/title/tt3521164/plotsummary

on't steal my

www.ingramcontent.com/pod-product-compliance
Lightning Source LLC
LaVergne TN
LVHW010935110826
845149LV00013B/2615

* 9 7 8 0 9 9 9 7 8 0 2 5 1 *